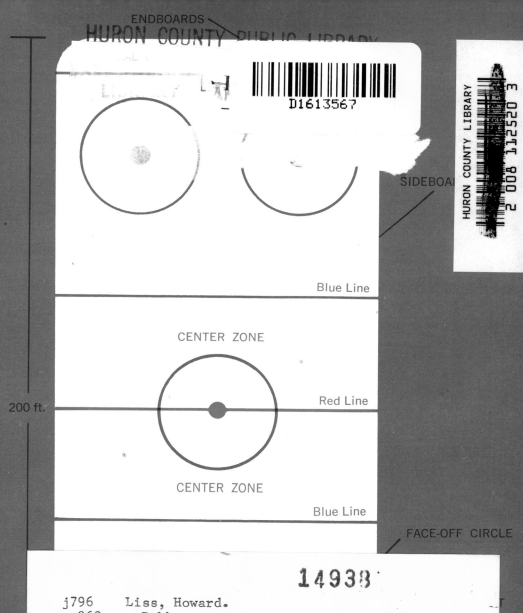

ENDBOARDS

SIDEBOARDS

Blue Line

CENTER ZONE

Red Line

CENTER ZONE

Blue Line

200 ft.

FACE-OFF CIRCLE

6

BOBBY ORR
LIGHTNING ON ICE

BY HOWARD LISS

ILLUSTRATED BY VICTOR MAYS

GARRARD PUBLISHING COMPANY
CHAMPAIGN, ILLINOIS

For Ricky Lesser—a great hockey fan

Sports Consultant:
COLONEL RED REEDER
Former Member of the West Point Coaching Staff
and Special Assistant to the West Point
Director of Athletics

Library of Congress Cataloging in Publication Data

Liss, Howard.
   Bobby Orr: lightning on ice.

    SUMMARY: A biography of Bobby Orr from the time he
learned to skate at age three until he became superstar
of the Boston Bruins.
    1. Orr, Bobby, 1948–   —Juvenile literature.
2. Hockey—Juvenile literature. [1. Orr, Bobby,
1948–   2. Hockey—Biography] I. Mays, Victor,
1927–   ill. II. Title.
GV848.5.O7L57   · 796.9′62′0924 [B] [92]   75–2423
ISBN 0–8116–6672–7

Photo credits:

Canada Wide from Pictorial Parade: pp. 33, 72 (top left), 76
United Press International: pp. 3, 43, 48, 57 (both),
   66 (both), 72 (top right and bottom right), 77,
   82 (both), 84 (bottom), 85, 86, 92, 95
Wide World Photos: pp. 60 (both), 72 (bottom left), 73, 79, 84 (top)

Contents

1. He's Too Small

It was a cold winter day in 1952. The Canadian town of Parry Sound, Ontario, was covered with a blanket of snow and ice. The nearby Seguin River was frozen into a solid sheet of ice. A small blond three-year-old boy named Bobby Orr stood on the riverbank. Beside him was his husky, broad-shouldered father, Doug Orr.

Doug laced a pair of skates on Bobby's feet. Then he put on his own skates and slid onto the ice.

"Come on, Bobby," he called. "It isn't hard to skate. You can do it."

Timidly, Bobby stepped onto the ice. At

first Doug Orr guided Bobby. He held his hand and pulled him along.

"Now try it alone," he said encouragingly to the boy. "If you fall, just get up and keep trying."

Bobby was unsteady, like any other boy who tries to ice-skate for the first time. His ankles bent inward, and his arms waved wildly. He took a stride forward, and, sure enough, he fell. Bobby got up and tried again. Once more he fell. But soon he could take several strides before falling. When they quit for the day, Bobby could skate quite well for a three year old.

Yet he had not done anything unusual. In Canada there are thousands of rivers, lakes, and ponds. Winter comes early, and the waters freeze solid. Almost all the boys and girls begin to skate when they are very young. Bobby's older brother, Ron, also learned at the age of three.

By the time Bobby was four, he was a good skater. He could race ahead faster than boys who were a year or two older. He began to play a game called *shinny*.

Shinny is played by almost all the youngsters in Canada and the northern part of the United States. There are almost no rules. A lot of boys just skate around the ice after a puck. Sometimes one "team" has a dozen players, and the other team has only ten. Nobody cares. The players try to keep possession of the puck as long as possible. Sometimes even a teammate will try to steal the puck away. About the only rule in the game is, "shinny on your own side." That means a player cannot switch to the other team during the game.

Even when he was four or five years old, Bobby was a good shinny player. He learned how to control the puck with his stick. Other players, bigger and older than

Bobby, would charge at him and try to take the puck away. Bobby would dodge and "deke," or he could flash away with a sudden burst of speed. (Deke means to fake a move in a different direction to fool the opponent.)

Soon Bobby wanted to play real hockey. In Canada there are hockey leagues for boys of all ages. In Parry Sound, for example, the youngest boys, under six years of age, play in the Minor Squirt division. As a boy gets older and gains experience, he goes on to the other divisions: Squirt, Pee Wee, Bantam, Midget, Junior, and Intermediate.

The Parry Sound games were played in the Memorial Community Center. It was an unheated building, but the spectators didn't mind. They enjoyed watching the youngsters play.

From the very beginning Bobby played

8

defense. He liked that position. Bobby was fast and could get away from opponents guarding him to score a lot of goals.

During the 1950s the Parry Sound teams were coached by a man named Bucko MacDonald. For years Bucko had been a fine defenseman with the Detroit Red Wings and Toronto Maple Leafs, clubs which belong to the National Hockey League. It was Bucko who taught Bobby some of the fundamentals of hockey.

"I knew Bobby would be great the first time I saw him skate," Bucko said later. "He was so easy to teach. When I told him what to do, he just went ahead and did it. And he never forgot anything."

Bobby's fast skating and stick handling soon made him a star of every division he played in. However, although Bobby was getting older, he was not getting much bigger. He was shorter and lighter than other boys his age. Bobby couldn't dodge all his opponents. Sometimes he was knocked down hard by the bigger boys.

In one fast game a hard spill left Bobby breathless on the ice. Coach MacDonald helped him to the sidelines.

"I think you'll be a great defenseman, Bobby," said Bucko. "You're small, kid, but you'll grow and put on weight. When you do, I think you'll become major-league material."

A worried Doug Orr was watching the game. "Maybe Bobby should switch to forward," he later suggested to the coach. "The boy is fast. He has a great shot on goal."

"No," said Bucko. "Defense is his natural position. Anybody can play forward, but not many players are good on defense. Bobby is the best defenseman for his age that I've ever seen."

Coach MacDonald realized that Bobby was a natural athlete and could be good at any sport. He was right. Bobby was a fast runner. He played lacrosse. He was a fine baseball player too. Bobby played short-stop. His speed enabled him to cover a lot of ground. At bat he cracked whizzing line drives through the infield.

When Bobby was eleven, he entered a schoolboy track meet and competed against boys who were eleven and twelve. Bobby won the sprints, some field events, and the middle-distance race. At the end of the meet, Bobby was given a trophy as the most outstanding athlete in the meet.

There was something extra special about that trophy. Twenty-five years earlier, the same kind of trophy had been won by Doug Orr, Bobby's father!

Bobby had inherited his all-around athletic ability from his grandfather and his father. Bobby's grandfather, for whom Bobby was named, had been a pro soccer star in his native Northern Ireland. When Grandfather Orr emigrated to Canada, he became a hockey fan.

Bobby's father, Doug Orr, had been an outstanding young hockey player. He played left wing. One night, when Doug was eighteen, the chief scout of the Boston Bruins watched him play. He wanted Doug to try out with one of Boston's farm teams, but Doug refused. World War II had begun, and he planned to join the navy.

During the war years, Doug served on a corvette, escorting supply ships across the Atlantic Ocean. By the time the war was over, he was married to a pretty girl named Arva Steele. Doug thought he was too old then to try out in pro hockey, so he returned to Parry Sound and got a job in an explosives factory. Robert Gordon

Orr, the third of Doug and Arva's five children, was born on March 20, 1948.

Growing up in Parry Sound was fun. In the summer, Bobby rode his bike and played baseball. There were plenty of other things to do outdoors too.

Bobby had a very special relationship with his grandfather. Often they would go for long hikes in the woods or go fishing for bass, sunfish, and pickerel.

In the winter months, when the river was frozen, Bobby spent long hours playing shinny and practicing with his hockey team.

Bobby's father never lost his love for hockey and still played occasionally. Once, when Bobby was about ten, Doug let Bobby and his brother, Ron, play on his grown-up team. Bobby surprised everyone by the way he handled the puck. He darted around the grown-ups, deking, dodging, and speeding away.

At the Gibson School, which Bobby attended in the seventh and eighth grades, he was known as an average student. His teachers liked him because he was so polite and respectful. Everyone else in Parry Sound liked Bobby too, and they were amazed that he had such athletic ability, in spite of his small size.

When Bobby was twelve, he played on the Parry Sound Bantam hockey team. He was only five feet, two inches tall and weighed 110 pounds, but Bobby was their star player. The team beat everyone in their area. At the end of the season the Parry Sound Bantams were invited to play in the All-Ontario Bantam championship tournament. It was to be held in a town called Guananoque, about 300 miles from Parry Sound.

Bobby didn't know it then, but his whole life was about to change.

2. Bantam Bobby Orr

When the All-Ontario tournament began, not many people outside Parry Sound knew how good a hockey player Bobby Orr was. By the time it was over, even some major-league scouts realized he would be a star some day.

In all other team sports, major-league scouts do not bother with twelve or thirteen year olds. The boys are still too young and too awkward to play good football, baseball, or basketball. But hockey is different, especially in Canada where it is the national sport.

Many Canadian boys join a hockey league when they are six or seven. By the time a boy is twelve, he has been playing hockey for a long time. A scout can often tell if he'll be pro material later on.

Watching the All-Ontario tournament were some scouts from the Boston Bruins. The Bruins had just finished a very bad season. For the first time in four years, Boston had failed to reach the Stanley Cup play-offs, the "World Series" of the National Hockey League. The scouts had to find some good new players who would help the Bruins in the future.

For the first few minutes the Boston scouts watched two boys they had heard about and had come especially to see. But soon they turned their attention to a small youngster playing defense for Parry Sound. The scouts could hardly believe their eyes. They saw the way Bobby stole the puck,

the way he shot at the goal. They were amazed at his speed.

"Look at that kid!" cried Lynn Patrick. He was then general manager of the Bruins.

"I guess you mean Number Two," said Milt Schmidt, Patrick's assistant. "He's great, but don't you think he's kind of small?"

Bobby helped his team win the game. Now they would face the Scarboro Lions for the championship. The scouts decided to watch the championship game too, to make sure that Number Two was as good as he looked.

After one period of the championship game, Lynn Patrick was convinced that Number Two was an outstanding player. "Find out more about that boy," he told scout Wren Blair.

In a few minutes Blair returned, smiling

broadly. "We must be the only ones here who never heard of him. His name is Bobby Orr. They say he's the best Bantam player in Ontario."

Parry Sound lost the championship game, 1-0. Bobby was outstanding. He played 58 of the game's 60 minutes. (For 2 minutes he was sent off the ice for a minor penalty.) When the game was over, the trophy for most valuable player in the tournament was voted to Bobby Orr.

"Is any team sponsoring the Parry Sound team?" asked Patrick anxiously.

"No," replied Wren Blair.

Good!" Patrick exclaimed. "Then we will."

In hockey in those days, a professional hockey league team often sponsored a young amateur team. The sponsoring team bought the amateur team's equipment. In return, the scouts of the sponsoring team had a chance to talk to the players' parents about pro contracts. Very often the parents were grateful for the sponsor's help, and their sons signed up with the sponsor's team.

Soon after the All-Ontario tournament, Wren Blair went to Parry Sound. He had a long talk with Doug Orr. Bobby would not be eligible to play big-league hockey until he was eighteen, but at fourteen he could sign with a Boston farm team. Four years after that he could sign with the Bruins. Blair wanted to make sure that Bobby would sign with the Boston farm team when he was older.

Bobby's father was not anxious to have his son play with the Boston Bruins. They were a United States team. Like almost everyone else in Parry Sound, Doug rooted for Toronto. Besides, Boston wasn't doing well. Doug wanted his son to play with a winning team.

Doug might have promised Bobby to the Toronto scout who came to Parry Sound later, but the scout made a mistake. Instead of talking to Doug Orr first, he spoke to Bobby's school principal. This angered Doug, and he said Bobby would never sign with Toronto. Many other scouts approached Doug, but he decided not to make any decisions yet.

For the next couple of years Wren Blair kept visiting the Orrs. Blair was coaching the Kingston, Ontario, team, which was a Boston farm club. Sometimes, when Kingston was traveling to play a game, Blair would have the bus go through Parry Sound, just so he could talk to the Orrs.

When Bobby reached the age of fourteen, Blair came to the Orr house again.

"Doug," he said, "I'd like Bobby to attend the Oshawa Generals' tryout camp."

Oshawa was a Boston farm team in a

Junior-A league. Junior-A hockey is pretty rough. A player has to be very good to stay in that league. Sometimes the best Junior-A players go right into the National Hockey League.

"Bobby is only fourteen," said Doug doubtfully. "Most of the players are from sixteen to eighteen, and they're much bigger than Bobby."

"Bobby will never improve if he keeps playing in Parry Sound," Blair replied. "He's better than anyone else in the area."

Finally Doug agreed. He realized that Bobby might get knocked around a bit, but that had happened before. The boy had never been hurt too badly.

More than 70 boys showed up at the Generals' tryout camp. They were among the best young players in Ontario.

When the boys saw Bobby and heard he played defense, they laughed. Bobby was still small and weighed only 127 pounds. To play that position in Junior-A, a boy had to be muscular, strong, and heavy. He had to be able to deliver a solid check to an opponent. As the boys watched slender Bobby glide around the ice for the first time, they thought one strong gust of wind would blow him into the boards.

But after one practice session, the laugh-

ing stopped. Bobby could skate hard and fast. He could fake and shoot. He handled his stick like a pro. Bobby charged in and broke up plays. He stole the puck and led the rush on goal. When the bigger boys cracked into him, Bobby took the check and gave one in return.

On the last day of the tryouts, Doug Orr came to the camp to take Bobby home. He

watched the practice game. Even he was amazed at Bobby's play. When the tryouts were over, Bobby Orr was voted the best of the 70 boys in camp.

"Doug, you must let Bobby play with Oshawa this year," Blair said.

"All right," Doug replied, "but there are two conditions. First, if I think the other players are too tough for Bobby to handle, the deal is off."

"Of course," Blair agreed. "We don't want him to get hurt."

"Also," Doug continued, "if Bobby's school marks drop, or if he gets sick, he won't play."

"That's fine with us," Blair nodded.

"Wait a minute," Doug smiled. "We haven't asked Bobby if he wants to play in Junior-A with the Generals."

"I'd like to try, dad," said Bobby. "I think I'm as good as they are."

So Bobby was signed with the Generals. When he reached the age of eighteen, he would play with Boston in the National Hockey League—if by that time he had proved that he was good enough.

Blair wanted his new recruit to live in Oshawa with a good family and go to school there. But Bobby's mother refused.

"The boy is only fourteen," she said. "He has never lived away from home. Oshawa is 150 miles from Parry Sound. We'd hardly ever see Bobby."

Doug Orr suggested that he drive Bobby from Parry Sound to Oshawa for each game. Then he would drive Bobby home right after the game.

"It's a long trip," Blair said as he finally agreed. "Bobby won't be able to practice with the team, and he's going to be tired."

"I know," replied Doug Orr grimly, "but we'll manage."

3. Junior-A Bobby

In some ways Bobby Orr's first year in Junior-A hockey was the most difficult of his entire career.

From Parry Sound to Oshawa, and then back to Parry Sound again, was a 300-mile round trip. Bobby and his father had to make the trip two or three times a week. Often, in the dead of winter, the roads were dangerous. Doug had to keep alert every mile of the way. He and Bobby were tired when they came home, but they couldn't get much sleep. Doug had to be up early to go to work. Bobby had to go to school.

Bobby had little chance to practice with his new teammates. He would arrive at the rink and suit up quickly. He could take just a few practice shots before the game started.

Bobby's teammates resented him at first. Why didn't he have to practice while they did? Why was he allowed to live at home while they couldn't? And why was Bobby getting so much publicity? Boston newspapers, as well as those in the Oshawa area, kept printing stories about him. Weren't they good players too?

Bobby's outstanding play soon won his teammates over. They began to appreciate the hardships he was going through. He never complained.

"The boy was terrific from the start," Wren Blair said later. "Bobby was barely into his teens. Yet he was playing better defense than anyone in the league."

In his first year with the Generals, Bobby scored six goals and had fifteen assists. He was voted to the second team of his league's all-star squad. Many fans thought he belonged on the first team.

When the season was over, the Orr family had a long talk about Bobby's future. It was too difficult for Doug and Bobby to keep making those long trips. Since Bobby would be fifteen years old next season, he was old enough to live away from home, they decided.

Wren Blair arranged for Bobby to live at the home of Mr. and Mrs. Robert Elsmere. The Bruins would pay for his food and lodging. Bobby would also receive ten dollars a week as spending money. That fall he enrolled at the R. S. McLaughlin Collegiate High School in Oshawa.

The Oshawa coaches were very strict with the boys living away from home.

When no game was scheduled the next day, the boys could stay up until 10:30. When there was a game the next day, bedtime was nine o'clock.

Sometimes Bobby broke those rules. He liked the Elsmeres and their three young children, but he missed his own family. Bobby telephoned home often, but that wasn't the same as seeing his parents and brothers and sisters. So, once in a while he hitched a ride to Parry Sound, to spend a few hours with his family. The Elsmeres understood how Bobby felt. When an Oshawa coach would call to check on Bobby, they would say he was asleep and should not be disturbed. Bobby was always back on time to go to school the following day. He never missed a game or a day of school because of those trips.

During this hockey season fifteen-year-old Bobby was able to practice with the team. Jim Cherry, the Generals' coach, worked with Bobby to sharpen his skills. Bobby learned how to position himself on defense in order to help the goalie. His skating improved. Bobby learned how to get started quickly and to skate even faster. His shots on goal became harder to stop.

His team play also improved. Bobby learned when to pass to his teammates, and they to him. That season Bobby scored 29 goals and had 43 assists. That would have been great for a center or wingman. For a defenseman like Bobby, it was superb.

After his second year Bobby was selected for the first team of the league's all-star squad. His fame spread all over Canada. Boston sportswriters began calling Bobby "The Million Dollar Beauty" and "Hockey's Hottest Prospect." Later, when

Bobby Orr in the uniform of the Oshawa Generals

Bobby moved to the home of Mr. and Mrs. Jack Wild, young hockey fans found out where he lived and hung around outside the house. They wanted to catch a glimpse of him.

But Bobby kept his modesty and good humor. When asked how it felt to be a teen-age celebrity, he replied, "I don't read that stuff about myself. I'm afraid I'm liable to get a swelled head."

It was the same old Bobby Orr when he went back to Parry Sound after the hockey season. He visited his friends, played ball, and went to the movies. As usual, he got a summer job. In past years he had worked at a butcher shop and for a summer hotel. This year he worked in a men's clothing store for $35 a week and often spent his entire salary buying clothes for himself. His family and friends teased him, but Bobby just smiled.

Summer was not all fun. Bobby knew he could never really succeed in hockey unless he added more muscle to his slender body. He began to exercise with barbells and handgrips to strengthen his wrists, arms, and shoulders. He developed powerful legs by running four miles a day.

The exercises helped tremendously. In his third season with the Generals, Bobby broke the scoring record for defensemen. He scored 34 goals and added 59 assists. The following year Bobby broke his own record. He scored 37 goals and was credited with 60 assists.

In 1966 the Russian national hockey team came to Canada on a goodwill tour. They played an exhibition game against a team of Junior-A all-stars. The Russians had the best amateur team in the world. They thought it would be an easy win against a team made up of teen-agers.

The Russians did win, 4–2, but it wasn't so easy. The junior team had some great players who would soon be in the National Hockey League. They included Derek Sanderson, destined for the Boston Bruins; Serge Savard, who would go to the Montreal Canadiens; Walt Tkaczuk, who would join the New York Rangers; and Danny Grant, bound for the Minnesota North Stars. Bobby Orr was on that team too. Bobby played a great game.

That winter, with Bobby leading the way, the Oshawa Generals won the Ontario Hockey Association Junior-A championship. Next they won the Eastern Canada Junior championship. Finally, the Generals took on the powerful Edmonton Oil Kings. The winner would take home the Memorial Cup for the junior championship of Canada.

It had been a long, hard season for eighteen-year-old Bobby. Other teams had learned that the only way to stop the Generals was by stopping Bobby Orr. He was a target for rival defensemen. When the series against the Oil Kings started, Bobby was suffering from a painful groin injury. He couldn't skate fast. At the end of five games, the Oil Kings were leading, three games to two. One more victory would give them the Memorial Cup.

Hap Emms, who had become the Boston general manager, went to see Bobby. "I don't want you to play," Emms said. "Your injury might get worse."

"I owe it to the guys," Bobby replied. "We've got to win the championship."

Doug Orr was there too. He looked anxiously at his son. "How do you feel, Bobby?" he asked.

"I'm okay, dad," Bobby insisted. "I want to play."

Doug was worried. He knew many fans

had come just to see Bobby in action, but he didn't want anything to happen to Bobby. Still, ever since Bobby had begun to play Junior-A hockey, Doug had felt that his son should make his own decisions.

Doug sighed. "All right, son," he said finally. "If that's what you want to do, I'll back you up."

Bobby did play. Because of his injury he couldn't really help the Generals. The Oil Kings won, but when he limped off the ice at the end of the game, the crowd stood and applauded.

The Bruins had been waiting impatiently for Bobby to reach the age of eighteen. Now he was eligible to play in the National Hockey League. The Bruins needed Bobby. For the past seven years they had failed to reach the Stanley Cup play-offs. Many fans had stopped attending home games. Perhaps Bobby could help bring them back.

Doug Orr knew little about contracts and could not advise Bobby. But he had once heard a lawyer named R. Alan Eagleson speak at a sports banquet, and he had liked what the young lawyer said. Eagleson had represented players with other teams. Doug decided that Eagleson was the best man to advise Bobby.

Eagleson drove a hard bargain. Finally the Bruins signed Bobby to a two-year contract. For those two years he would be paid about $50,000—not bad for an eighteen-year-old!

Bobby had a great contract. Now he had to prove that he was worth his salary.

4. Major-League Rookie

It was a different Bobby Orr who re-
ported to the Boston Bruins at the start of
the 1966–67 season. The years of exercise
and the miles of roadwork had paid off. All
of a sudden—or so it seemed—he had
grown up and put on weight. Now, at the
start of his rookie season, he was five feet,
eleven inches tall and weighed 175 pounds.
Most of the major-league defensemen were
heavier, some weighing 200 pounds or
more. But at least Bobby had the size and
weight to take care of himself against
tough opposition.

At first the Boston players couldn't understand what kind of person Bobby was. He had received a lot of publicity. They expected him to boast about his contract and to brag how good he was, but Bobby called his new teammates "mister" and "sir." They thought he was kidding them. Then they found out that Bobby really was a modest young man. They liked him for that.

For the first time the Boston coaches could study Bobby's style. They watched him closely in every game. Mostly, the coaches liked what they saw, but they realized Bobby still needed work in the fundamentals of hockey.

The coaches liked his skating style. Bobby skated with his feet far apart, which gave him good balance. It took a hard shove to knock him off his feet. They also noted how quickly he started. It took most skaters four or five steps before they were in full stride. Bobby needed only a step or two, and then he was away at top speed. One admiring teammate watched him zoom down the ice, picking up steam with every flash of his blades. He said, "That kid has fifteen different speeds of fast."

Those were some of Bobby's good points, but he made mistakes too. For instance, he

The Bruins' teen-age wonder (second from right) lines up with his teammates at Boston Garden.

was shooting too high. Some of his shots on goal bounced off the crossbar on top of the net.

"I know what's wrong. I'm not following through properly," Bobby told the coaches. He worked hard to get his shots down lower.

Bobby was fooled by experienced forwards. Because he kept his eyes on the puck, he was wide open for a quick fake or a fast dodge around him. The coaches told Bobby to watch his opponent's chest.

Wren Blair gave Bobby some advice about fighting. "Sometimes there are a lot of fights in a game," he said to Bobby.

"I know," Bobby smiled. "I guess it's because hockey is such a fast game. The players check each other hard. They lose their tempers and start punching."

"Don't back away from anyone," Blair warned the budding young star. "A lot of players will test you, to see if you are tough enough for big-league hockey. They will try to get you into a fight. If you back away, they will make your life miserable. Fight back!"

Bobby was tested soon enough. Tough Ted Harris of Montreal picked a fight with him during a game. Bobby reacted swiftly. With a flip of his hands, Bobby threw his gloves into Harris's face. Then, before Harris could recover, Bobby knocked him down. The officials quickly broke up the fight and play continued.

Another time a rough player named Reg Fleming went after Bobby. They shouted angrily at each other. Suddenly Fleming hit Bobby in the nose. They were separated before any more punches could be thrown. Bobby kept sniffling because he didn't want Fleming to see that his punch had drawn blood. A few minutes later,

Bobby checked Fleming into the boards, hard.

After the game Fleming said, "The kid can take it, and he can dish it out, too. I respect him for that."

Bobby proved he could fight back, but he still made mistakes. They were the kind any rookie might make. In one game he started down the ice with the puck when he heard a voice call, "Drop it! Drop it!" Bobby thought it was a teammate who wanted him to make a drop pass. Bobby stopped the puck, left it behind, and skated away so his teammate could get it. But the voice belonged to an opponent. Bobby had been fooled.

In another game an experienced forward came right at Bobby. He faked once, faked twice, and as Bobby was trying to figure out what was happening, the forward shot the puck through Bobby's legs for a goal.

But Bobby didn't let such things happen too often. In only his second game, he scored his first major-league goal. The game was against Montreal. Streaking down the ice, Bobby let fly with a blazing slap shot. The puck went into the net before the goalie could move to block it.

Boston fans loved Bobby. When he made a good play, they cheered. When an opponent fouled him, they booed the player. Once an opponent hooked Bobby and was given a two-minute penalty.

"Hey, ref, make that two minutes and thirty seconds," shouted an angry Boston rooter. "Two minutes for hooking, and an extra thirty seconds because it was Bobby Orr!"

Bobby's teammates felt the same way about him. One of his chief admirers was defenseman Ted Green. Watching Bobby streak across the ice, feinting, dodging,

**Bobby defends his goal against Montreal
as Bruin Jerry Cheevers freezes the puck.**

and passing, Green said, "Kid, I don't know how much they're paying you, but it's not enough."

Fans and sportswriters began comparing Bobby with two of the greatest defensemen ever to play hockey. One was Eddie Shore, who had also played with the Bruins. The other was Doug Harvey, who had played with Montreal's great championship teams.

Boston coach Harry Sinden refused to take part in that discussion. He said, "Bobby Orr should not be compared with Shore or Harvey. Remember, when Shore was playing, no forechecking was allowed." (Forechecking means checking into an opponent in his own defensive zone.) "When Eddie got the puck he had plenty of time to start a rush. But the rules were changed. Bobby does get checked in his own defensive zone."

Then Sinden added, "Besides, Shore had

some good moves that Bobby still doesn't have."

As for Doug Harvey, Sinden said that the former Montreal ace controlled the puck better than Bobby. Harvey got the offensive rush moving much quicker. But Bobby was still a rookie, and he scored more goals than Harvey.

Some opposing players thought Bobby was trying to score too often. They said he might be hurting the Bruins that way.

Bobby Hull, the Black Hawks' superstar, said, "Because Orr rushes so deep into the other team's zone, he's often caught out of position. He doesn't have time to get back into his own defensive zone. The other defenseman is all alone. He has to handle two forwards coming at him."

Emile Francis, boss of the Rangers, disagreed with Hull. Francis said, "I try to think how many times we've caught Orr out of position and scored a goal. It didn't happen very often."

Red Kelly, who had been an all-time great player, thought Bobby would be a superstar soon. "I've never seen a weakness in Orr," Kelly said. "He has the puck about 75 percent of the time. If he has the puck, the other team can't score. That's the best kind of defense."

Since Bobby was such a good scorer, Boston officials thought he might be better off as a forward.

For a few games Bobby was switched to center. He did quite well at the new position, but he didn't like it. Soon he was back on defense.

"I wasn't happy at center," he told a sportswriter. "On defense you're facing the play all the time. You can't do that on the forward line. I like to know where the puck is."

Coach Sinden agreed. "It wasn't a smart switch," he said. "Bobby can become a fine center, but he's the best defenseman in the league right now. Where would we get anyone to replace him on defense?"

So Bobby remained a defenseman. He had an outstanding season in 1966–67. In 61 games he scored 13 goals and had 28 assists.

Boston sportswriters pointed out that the great Jean Beliveau had also scored 13 goals as a rookie, but that he had only 21 assists. The fantastic Gordie Howe banged home 7 goals in his first year, and had 15 assists. Bobby Hull scored 13 goals and picked up 34 assists as a rookie.

They were forwards, while Bobby was a defenseman. Other defensemen in the league took notice. Maybe they too should try scoring more often. Bobby Orr was starting to change the strategy of hockey.

Bobby Orr won the Calder Trophy as Rookie of the Year. He was named to the second team of the National Hockey League all-star squad.

That same year Harry Howell, the New York Rangers star, won the James Norris Trophy. That is the award given to the best defensive player in the league. Howell smiled and said, "I'm glad I won it now, because Bobby Orr is going to win it for the next ten years."

In spite of his award, Bobby wasn't completely happy. The Bruins had failed to get into the Stanley Cup play-offs again. Even his splendid play had not been enough.

But the Bruins had made a fine start. The team needed just a few more good players to build up their strength. Next year there would be new faces, to help Bobby take the Boston Bruins along the road to the championship.

5. Injuries

After his rookie season was over, Bobby went back to Parry Sound. He was a hero to his family and friends, but in his heart Bobby knew his success was due partly to luck. He had been playing hockey since he was five and had never been seriously injured.

Bobby had played many sports. He knew that hockey was the roughest team sport of all. Every player in pro hockey has been hurt many times. Almost all had lost a few teeth, and many had broken bones. Yet Bobby had escaped with just some painful bumps and bruises and a few cuts. They had not bothered him much.

In the summer of 1967 Bobby's luck ran out. He played in a charity game for the benefit of old-time hockey players. In one wild scramble Bobby was knocked into the boards. He injured his knee.

For five weeks Bobby's knee was in a cast. When the cast was taken off, his knee seemed strong again. But early in the season, in a game against the Maple Leafs, Bobby was hit hard on the same knee. He had to spend ten days in the hospital. When he returned to action, the knee was still stiff and sore.

The Bruins were especially unhappy about Bobby's injury because they had begun to rebuild the team. They had looked to Bobby as the leader of the new players.

From junior hockey came a tough fighter named Derek Sanderson. Two years earlier, he had played on the same team with

Bobby against the touring Russian team. Sanderson was always ready for a fight. In one game he got angry at an opponent who was 20 pounds heavier. Sanderson knocked him out with a single punch, but he was punished later. After the game, half a dozen fans cornered him in the dressing room and thrashed him soundly.

Milt Schmidt, who was now the Bruins' general manager, made a great trade with Chicago. Boston received centers Phil Esposito and Fred Stanfield, plus wingman Ken Hodge.

Unfortunately for the Bruins, Bobby was in and out of the lineup that year. In December of 1967, an opponent crashed into Bobby and knocked him down with a loud thud. It was a legal check, but that didn't make Bobby feel any better. He fractured his collarbone and suffered a shoulder separation.

Bobby races Chicago's Pit Martin for the
puck (above) and smashes one into the net
past the Toronto goalie (below).

Bobby remained on the sidelines for a while. But when he was named to the first team of the all-star squad, he insisted on playing in the All-Star Game. In spite of his aches he played a great game.

After the All-Star Game, Bobby hurt his knee again. This time he could not hide the pain. He flew back to Boston for a knee operation. The doctors said the operation was successful, but Bobby had to take it easy for a while.

For the first time in many years Boston had a chance to reach the Stanley Cup play-offs. About a month after his operation, Bobby said he was ready to play. He really wasn't, and Coach Sinden knew it. Bobby was rusty. He hadn't played for a long time. But even when he wasn't up to par, Bobby was a better defenseman than most others in the league.

Bobby returned to action against the

Detroit Red Wings. He helped the Bruins win that game. Boston went on to finish third in the Eastern Division. They had reached the play-offs at last!

The Stanley Cup play-offs involve the first four teams of the Eastern and Western Divisions of the National Hockey League. In each division, the four teams are paired off. The teams play a series, and the winner of four games wins that series. This leaves two teams in each division. Once more a series is played, and the team winning four games wins the series.

Finally, the winner in the Eastern Division plays the winner in the Western Division. The team winning four games is champion of the National Hockey League and gets the Stanley Cup.

Boston played the powerful Montreal Canadiens. Montreal squeaked out the first game, 2–1. They also won the next three.

**Phil Esposito (left) and Derek Sanderson
(right) beefed up the Bruins' line in 1967.**

The Bruins tried hard, but they just
weren't good enough.

Even though they had been eliminated
quickly, the season was not a complete
failure for Boston. The new players had
been outstanding. Derek Sanderson won

60

the Calder Trophy as Rookie of the Year, just as Bobby had won it the year before. Phil Esposito, the new center, made some great shots on goal. That season he finished second in the league in scoring. Most important of all, the Bruins had finally reached the Stanley Cup play-offs.

It had been a spectacular season for Bobby, in spite of his injuries. He played in only 44 games, but still managed to score 11 goals and 20 assists. Many major-league defensemen who played the whole season would have been glad to achieve such a fine record.

Harry Howell's prediction came true. Bobby won the James Norris Trophy as best defenseman in the league.

At last Bobby Orr was a full-fledged star.

6. Bobby Orr: Star

In spite of Bobby's operation, his knee was still stiff and sore. X rays showed a loose chip of cartilage. Another operation was performed to remove it.

Now Bobby and his lawyer had to make an important decision. Bobby's contract with the Bruins had expired. How much should they ask for this season? Alan Eagleson was determined that Bobby would be paid what he was really worth to the team.

Bobby Orr was one of the greatest attractions in hockey, the lawyer pointed out. He drew as many fans in Boston as

Bobby Hull did in Chicago, or Gordie Howe in Detroit, and Eagleson could prove it.

During Bobby's rookie year, Boston had failed to reach the play-offs. Yet the team drew 44,000 more fans to Boston Garden than they did the year before. Other teams also had bigger crowds than usual when Boston came to their cities. Clearly, the reason was Bobby Orr. Attendance had increased again during Bobby's second year.

It took a long time, but finally Bobby and the Bruins agreed to terms. The exact amount of money was not made public, but most sportswriters thought Bobby got about $400,000 over the next three years.

Bobby's teammates were not jealous. Indeed, they were very pleased. So were other stars in the league. For Bobby Orr had cracked through the "$100,000 barrier."

Before Bobby's contract, hockey salaries

were low compared with those in baseball, football, and basketball. In those sports many stars were paid $100,000 a year, and in some cases much more. But no one in hockey had ever been paid that much, not even the great Gordie Howe or Bobby Hull.

Others began to demand more money. One player said, "I'm about half as good as Bobby Orr, so I should get half as much money as he's getting. That would mean double my salary!"

The players were grateful to Bobby's lawyer, for he had helped them all. He was elected head of the players' association.

Meanwhile, in the 1968–69 season, Bobby had to prove he was worth his high salary. His knee had mended, and he was skating beautifully, but his opponents slammed into him harder than ever.

During the first of two games against

Montreal, Bobby got a cut over one eye, which took five stitches to close. Next morning the eye was swollen shut. Bobby went to the Bruins dressing room early and had hot packs put on the eye. After about an hour it was partly open. Bobby suited up and started playing hockey.

Bobby could see properly out of only one eye, but that didn't stop him. With the score tied at 4–all, he grabbed the puck. He took off down the ice on a solo dash. Blocking his path was tough Ted Harris. Bobby cut around and went behind the goal with Harris chasing him. Then he pivoted in front of the net and fired in the puck for the go-ahead score. Boston won that game.

A couple of weeks later Bobby came down with the flu. He felt terrible, but he insisted on playing. As usual Bobby did a great job. He scored an important goal,

In action against the Rangers in 1969:
Bobby tears away from defensemen (above)
and breaks up a drive on the goal (below).

which helped the Bruins beat the Rangers, 4–2.

On March 20, with the season just about over, Bobby gave his admirers more cause to cheer. Boston was losing, 5–4. Bobby got the puck and streaked off on a break-away rush. There was no time to pass to a teammate. Bobby drove in and smashed the puck into the net to tie the game. There were just three seconds left to play when he scored!

It was his 21st goal of the season. That broke the record for scoring by a defense-man, which had been set by Flash Hollett of Detroit, back in 1944–45.

The Bruins finished in second place in the Eastern Division. As usual, Montreal finished first. Still, the Bruins had scored 100 points, more than any other Boston team had ever scored. (In hockey, a vic-tory counts as 2 points and a tie game as

1 point.) Bobby had broken the scoring record for defensemen, with 21 goals and 43 assists. Also, Bobby won the Norris Trophy for the second year in a row.

The 1969 Stanley Cup play-offs were exciting. Boston played Toronto in the opening series and clobbered them in four straight games. In the first game Boston won, 10–0. Phil Esposito scored four goals.

It was a rough day for Bobby. In the second period big Pat Quinn knocked him flat. Bobby lay on the ice in a daze. To his disappointment, he was out of the game.

Boston won the second game, 7–0. Bobby did not play much, but he wasn't needed. The Bruins eliminated Toronto by winning the next two games, 4–3 and 3–2.

Then it was Boston against Montreal. It was slam-bang action all the way. Montreal won the first two games, 3–2 and 4–3. But they had to play overtime in both.

Back came Boston to win the next two games on home ice. It was Bobby Orr leading the way. The Bruins won the third game, 5-0. Bobby had two assists. They won the fourth game, 3-2. Bobby Orr scored the winning goal.

But that was as far as Boston could go. Montreal rallied to win the next two games, 4-2 and 2-1.

"Next year!" growled Derek Sanderson. "We're going to win that Stanley Cup next year."

Bobby and the rest of the Bruins nodded. Somehow they just knew that they would be champions the following year.

7. The Championship

A long line of youngsters stood outside Boston Garden. They were waiting for the Bruins to come out of the dressing room. They wanted autographs.

Like all the other players, Bobby signed his name cheerfully. Then he noticed one of the boys getting back in line again and again. When the boy reached him for the third time, Bobby asked why he wanted so many autographs.

"We trade them," the boy replied. "My dad said some day your autograph will be worth more than any of the others."

Young girls also waited to see Bobby. One girl had to use a wheelchair. She came to the Garden frequently, and Bobby always walked over to her. Their greeting was usually the same.

"Hi," she would say to Bobby. "Got any new girl friends lately?"

"Nope. I'm waiting for you," Bobby would answer and stoop to kiss her on the cheek.

One night, after he had left the young girl, he said to a friend, "I'm so lucky. I have my health. I love to play hockey, and I get paid for it. But look at that poor kid in a wheelchair. I feel so sorry for her."

Bobby was both thoughtful and generous. Everyone knew about the beautiful home he was building for his family. They also knew that Bobby was honorary chairman of the muscular dystrophy fund-raising drive in Canada. He worked for the March of

It's All Part of the Game

Bobby skates with young friends . . .

warms the bench . . .

talks things over with fans . . .

gets a pat on the back
from Coach Sinden . . .

checks his sticks just before game time.

Dimes and the United Fund in Boston. He often visited hospitals and orphanages.

Bobby liked to go to a certain restaurant for cheeseburgers and a bottle of beer. He became friends with Tommy Maher, the bartender there. Maher often asked Bobby for some of his old equipment. He would auction the things off and give the money to charity. A pair of Bobby's skates brought $1,000.

Bobby gave a lot of his own money to charity. He also donated his clothes, usually to the Sacred Heart parish in nearby Watertown. Bobby wasn't a Catholic, but he respected all religions.

Once a Boston fan's car was caught on a patch of ice. A man in the car behind got out and pushed the stuck driver's car. "Thanks," the grateful driver called out. Then he saw who had pushed him off the ice. It was Bobby.

"That's OK," Bobby said. "I know you'd have done the same for me."

Fame had not changed Bobby. He was still polite to everyone. He always laughed and joked with his teammates. But when a game started, the politeness and the jokes were forgotten. He became a tough hockey player, the best defenseman in the National Hockey League.

All Bobby's accomplishments in the past were just a warm-up for the 1969–70 season. With the opening face-off of the season, Bobby went on a scoring spree. He piled up goals and assists. Soon he was leading the league in points scored.

Bobby's skating, stick handling, and shooting seemed to improve with each game. One night, against Montreal, he was trapped between two big defensemen who wanted to "make a sandwich" of him. Bobby faked once, twice—then suddenly turned on a burst of speed. The defense-men crashed into each other. Bobby scored.

Another weekend the Bruins played the Rangers and Los Angeles on successive days. In the Rangers game Bobby showed more fancy stick handling. As he came in on goalie Ed Giacomin, Bobby faked to the left, then to the right. While Giacomin was trying to figure out which way Bobby was

Bobby blazes past a Montreal opponent . . .

going, he left a corner of the net open. Bobby rifled in a slap shot.

A few minutes later Bobby intercepted a pass at the Rangers' blue line. With one swift motion he let fly at the goal. Score again!

The next day, against Los Angeles, Bobby had four assists. Thus, in two days, Bobby had six points.

and whips the puck into Montreal's net.

Fans began to wonder if league-leading Bobby might score as many as 100 points during the season. Once it had been an impossible dream for a defenseman, but that was before Bobby Orr came into the league.

Bobby reached that total in a 5–5 tie game against Detroit. The 100th point was not made during a particularly exciting play. Bobby just happened to be in the right place at the right time.

"How about that Bobby Orr," said a Boston fan to a Detroit fan after the game. "Isn't he terrific!"

"Why don't you wait until he's been playing a few years longer," snapped the Detroit rooter.

"Yeah," chuckled the Boston fan. "Just think how great he'll be then."

Bobby didn't stop at 100 points. He added more goals and more assists. He

**Bobby becomes the first defenseman in the
National Hockey League to score 100 points
and gets a bear hug from his teammates.**

collected 33 goals and 87 assists for a total of 120 points. Bobby Orr became the first defenseman to lead the National Hockey League in scoring!

It was Boston against New York as the Eastern teams battled each other in the opening Stanley Cup series. The first game was close for one period. Boston led, 2–1. Early in the second period, Bobby flashed in on the net. He took his shot. The puck hit a sidepost and skittered away. Bobby went after it and shot again. Score! Now it was 3–1.

Later in the same game one of the Bruins went to the penalty box. The team was one man short. Bobby skated around aimlessly with the puck. He wanted the Rangers to think he was killing time until his teammate returned. Suddenly he took off like a streak of lightning. He darted through the center of the rink and banged the puck into the Rangers' net. Boston won that game, 8–2.

The Bruins also won the second game, 5–3. Bobby was credited with an assist.

New York bounced back to capture the next two games and tie the series, but Bobby managed to score a goal in each game.

Bobby showed a new trick in the fifth game. As the teams were changing lines, he suddenly jack-rabbited toward the Rangers' goal. Before the Rangers could try to stop him, he had scored. Teammate Phil Esposito scored two goals and Boston won, 3–2.

Boston eliminated the Rangers in the next game with a 3–1 victory. Bobby scored a pair of goals. That broke the record for goals scored by a defenseman in Stanley Cup competition. Before, Earl Siebert and Red Kelly had been tied with

The 1970 Stanley Cup play-offs: Bobby
sneaks one past Chicago goaltender Tony
Esposito (above) and, in another game, is
upended by Ranger Jim Neilson.

six goals. But Siebert took ten games to get his half-dozen goals, and Kelly needed twelve. Bobby had scored seven goals in six games!

When the series was over, Ranger coach Emile Francis told reporters, "Bobby Orr beat us. Great—that's the only word I can use to describe him."

Then Boston played Chicago for the Eastern Division title. It was a hard series, but Boston was not to be stopped. They beat Chicago in four straight games. Now only the Saint Louis Blues stood between Boston and the Stanley Cup.

The first three games were comparatively easy victories for Boston. But the fourth game was a battle every minute. After three periods the teams were tied at 3-all.

Less than a minute into overtime, there was a scramble near the Saint Louis goal.

Bobby flips over the back of a St. Louis player (above) as he is checked in the third period. Below, he has just scored the goal that wins the Stanley Cup for the Bruins.

Suddenly the puck flew out of the tangle. It went straight to Bobby, who was stationed near the Saint Louis blue line. He charged in, got possession, and passed to Sanderson. Then Bobby bored in on the goal. Sanderson passed back to him. Goal! The Boston Bruins had finally won the Stanley Cup, after 29 long years. There was a wild, champagne-spilling celebration in the dressing room.

Bobby celebrates with a shower of champagne.

Bobby is a star on and off the ice! Boston
fans mob him in the Bruins' victory parade.

The 1969–70 season had been fantastic
for Bobby. He became the first player ever
to win *four* trophies in a single season.

He won the Art Ross Trophy for leading
the league in scoring.

He won the Norris Trophy as best defenseman for the third time in a row.

He won the Hart Trophy as the Most
Valuable Player in the league.

He won the Conn Smythe Trophy as Most Valuable Player in Stanley Cup competition.

Bobby also won the *Sport* magazine award as "Man Of The Year."

And he won $17,750 in bonuses in individual and team awards.

Bobby had set many other records. He was the first defenseman to score 100 points. His 87 assists in one season was also a record. He had scored 20 points in Stanley Cup play—9 goals and 11 assists. That was a record for defensemen. And, of course, his winning four trophies was another record.

Bobby was the idol of Boston fans. One rooter said, "Maybe they should change the rules and elect Bobby Orr to the Hockey Hall of Fame while he's still playing."

Yet Bobby had been in the major league for only four years.

8. Bobby Orr: Superstar

"If there is a new way to beat you, Bobby Orr will find it."

That was what fans and sportswriters were saying about Boston's great young defenseman. It wasn't merely that he could skate, shoot, and block out an opponent. Bobby was always using his head. He could think of his next move in a split second.

In a game against Minnesota, Bobby intercepted a pass near the Minnesota goal. Goalie Cesare Maniago braced for Bobby's shot. Bobby drew back his stick and fired, but it wasn't a shot on goal. Instead, he passed hard to Esposito, standing near the other corner of the net. Esposito poked the puck in. One more assist for Bobby!

In a game against Philadelphia, Bobby stole the puck and streaked goalward. Three Philadelphia players chased him. Suddenly Bobby stopped short. The three players went right by him. Bobby's shot on goal was blocked. A moment later, after a face-off, Bobby got the puck again. He shot. Score one more goal for Bobby!

In a game against Saint Louis, the Bruins were one man short because of a penalty. The Blues worked a power play. Bobby backed up near his own goal. As the shot came, Bobby swept his stick to the side and blocked it, but the hard shot knocked the stick from his hands. The puck skidded to another Blues player. Without his stick, Bobby rushed into the play. As the Saint Louis player was about to shoot, Bobby kicked the puck away with his skate. Then he chased the puck, caught it, and froze the puck against the boards with his skate. The power play was stopped by Bobby Orr—*without* a stick in his hands!

Bobby and Boston had another great season in 1970–71. The Bruins finished first in the Eastern Division. Their 57 victories in one season was a record. They scored 121 points. The team scored 399 goals.

Bobby Orr's 102 assists broke his own record. Bobby's 139 points was a new record for a defenseman. Several other Bruins set individual records too. Phil Esposito had 76 goals, the most ever scored by a player. He had a total of 152 points, the most ever scored by a player. Johnny Bucyk and Ken Hodge also scored more than 100 points each.

But Boston was not destined to win the Stanley Cup. The Montreal Canadiens put them out in seven hard games. Boston fans were stunned. What had happened?

First, the Montreal goalie, Ken Dryden, guarded the net in great style. He was one of the reasons Montreal won the Stanley Cup that year.

Second, Montreal "shadowed" Bobby with a left winger all night. Wherever Bobby went, the left winger went. Bobby was checked hard, tied up, tired out.

As usual, Bobby won his share of awards that season. He won the Norris Trophy again. He won the Hart Trophy again, and he won the Lou Marsh Trophy as "Canada's best athlete."

The Bruins swept into the 1971–72 season determined to win *everything*, and they did. They finished at the top of the Eastern Division. They won the Stanley Cup. It was another magnificent year for Bobby Orr.

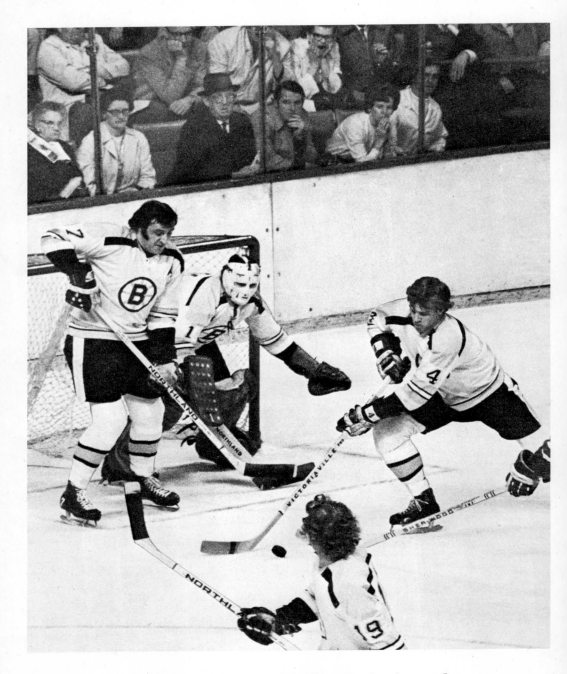

First line of defense! Bobby whisks the puck away from the Bruin net into safer territory.

He scored 37 goals and had 80 assists for 117 points. It was the third straight year he scored more than 100 points. Once it was thought impossible for a defenseman to score half that many points. Now Bobby was scoring over 100 every season!

Bobby won the Norris Trophy again. He won the Hart Trophy again.

But Bobby's knee, injured long ago in that charity game, was bothering him. He had to undergo another operation. As a result, Bobby missed the first fourteen games of the 1972-73 season. Yet he scored more than 100 points again, with 29 goals and 72 assists. And for the *sixth* year in succession Bobby won the Norris Trophy as best defenseman.

Bobby Orr had his usual great season in 1973-74. He finished second in the league in scoring, with 32 goals and 90 assists for a total of 122 points. Once more, he won the Norris Trophy as the league's best defenseman. Boston finished first in the Eastern Division, but the Philadelphia Flyers won the Stanley Cup, beating the Bruins in the finals of the play-offs.

Some fans insist that Bobby Orr is the greatest hockey player of all time, regardless of position. They claim Boston could never win without him. Others disagree. They point to other players who have helped Boston win the Stanley Cup, such as Esposito, Hodge, Bucyk, and Cashman. The Bruins have been a great *team*.

There are two answers to that argument. One was supplied by Rod Gilbert, the Rangers star. After Boston had beaten the Rangers in the 1970 play-offs, Gilbert said, "Hockey is a team game, right? One man is not supposed to beat a whole team, right? But what else can I say? You saw it. Bobby Orr beat the Rangers."

Bobby Orr, pride of the Bruins—a super-star for the seventies.

The other answer was supplied by Bobby Orr himself. The Bruins had just beaten Saint Louis for the Stanley Cup. Bobby had scored the winning goal. In the dressing room, reporters and teammates were shaking his hand and slapping him on the back.

Bobby said, "It wasn't me who scored the winning goal. The credit belongs to ten guys—the team—these guys I play with are unbelievable—just unbelievable!"

Is Bobby Orr greater than Eddie Shore or Doug Harvey, the superstar defensemen of years ago? That is hard to answer. But one thing is certain: Bobby Orr is the greatest defenseman of *his own* time.

PROFESSIONAL
ICE HOCKEY RINK

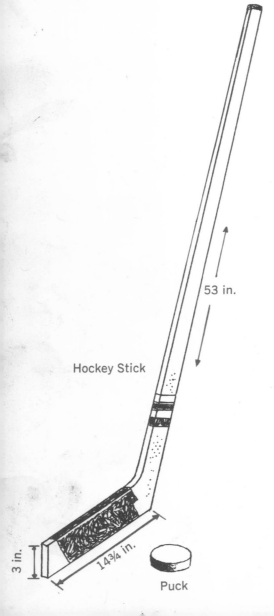

Hockey Stick

53 in.

14¾ in.

3 in.

Puck

Professional ice hockey is usually played on a rectangular ice rink measuring about 200 feet long and 85 feet wide. The measurements, however, vary somewhat from rink to rink.

A goal cage is placed 10 feet in from each end of the rink. The goal cage consists of 2 upright posts, 4 feet high and 6 feet apart, and a net which extends from the top of the posts down to the ice. The net encloses the sides and back, forming a cage. A red goal line is painted on the ice to connect the bases of the posts. In front of each goal is a rectangular area which measures 8 by 4 feet. This area is called the crease.

Around the ice is a white wooden wall 3½ to 4 feet high. Behind the goals the wall is called the endboards; at the sides of the rink, it is called the sideboards.

Two blue lines are drawn on the ice dividing the rink into 3 equal playing areas: the center zone, the offensive zone, and the defensive zone. A red center line divides the rink into 2 equal parts.

There are 5 face-off spots, one in the exact center of the rink and 2 in each end zone. They are surrounded by a blue face-off circle with a radius of 15 feet.

The wooden hockey stick, consisting of a handle with a blade at the end, may not exceed 53 inches in length. The blade itself may not exceed 14¾ inches in length. The height of the blade may not exceed 3 inches except for the goalkeeper's, which may be 3½ inches in height.

The puck is a vulcanized rubber disk, 1 inch thick and 3 inches in diameter.